1998

Blue Peter Stamp Annual

Belongs to :

Stick your photo here!

1998 Blue Peter Stamp Annual.
Devised, edited & designed by Yellow Submarine Publishing.
All rights reserved.
Illustrations by Jody Winger.
Photography by Chris Capstick.

Yellow Submarine Publishing is an imprint of
The Yellow Submarine Promotional Marketing Consultants Ltd.
© Copyright 1997 The Yellow Submarine Promotional Marketing Consultants Ltd.

Blue Peter © & ™ BBC 1985. Blue Peter logo BBC 1963.
Licensed by BBC Worldwide Ltd.

Published by Yellow Submarine Publishing,
Dry Dock, 17a West Street, EPSOM, Surrey, KT18 7RL

ISBN 0 9530701 0 7

All rights reserved.
No part of this publication may be reproduced,
stored in a retrieval system, or transmitted,
in any form or by any means, electronic, mechanical,
photocopying, recording or otherwise,
without the prior written permission of the publishers.

Printed in Italy by Vallardi Industrie Grafiche S.p.a.

THE
YELLOW SUBMARINE

Contents

An Introduction from the Blue Peter Team   4

1998 Special Stamp Issues   6

How to Collect Stamps   8

1998 Year Planner with Special Stamp Collecting Pages   10

General Stamp Collecting Pages   52

Names and Addresses   60

Notes   64

1997, 1998 & 1999 Calendars   69

Acknowledgements   72

Welcome to the brand new Blue Peter Stamp Annual and an exciting year of British Special Stamps. We are always interested in the subjects of Special Stamps and look forward to novel ways of featuring them on the show. Recently, this has led to Stuart dressing up as Henry VIII and to us scaring each other with Dracula and Frankenstein costumes!

Each year Royal Mail releases about nine sets of Special Stamps - and 1998 is no exception. With exciting subjects such as Endangered Species, Speed - (*honouring great British speed record holders*), and Carnival, 1998 promises to be another great year.

The new Blue Peter Stamp Annual is a superb way of collecting these stamps. With fascinating facts on each of the stamp issues and a diary page for each month, the Blue Peter Stamp Annual will become a very personal keepsake to look back on in years to come!

Keep the annual safe and you will be able to re-read it year after year remembering not only what you did during 1998 but also admiring your Special Stamp Collection.

Have a fun year and keep watching Blue Peter for more details of the Special Stamp releases!

- *Romana wonders if these wives of Henry VIII were divorced or beheaded!... Stuart tries to give her a clue.*
- *Katy comes face-to-face with Frankenstein!*
- *Richard gets under the bonnet of his favourite car!*

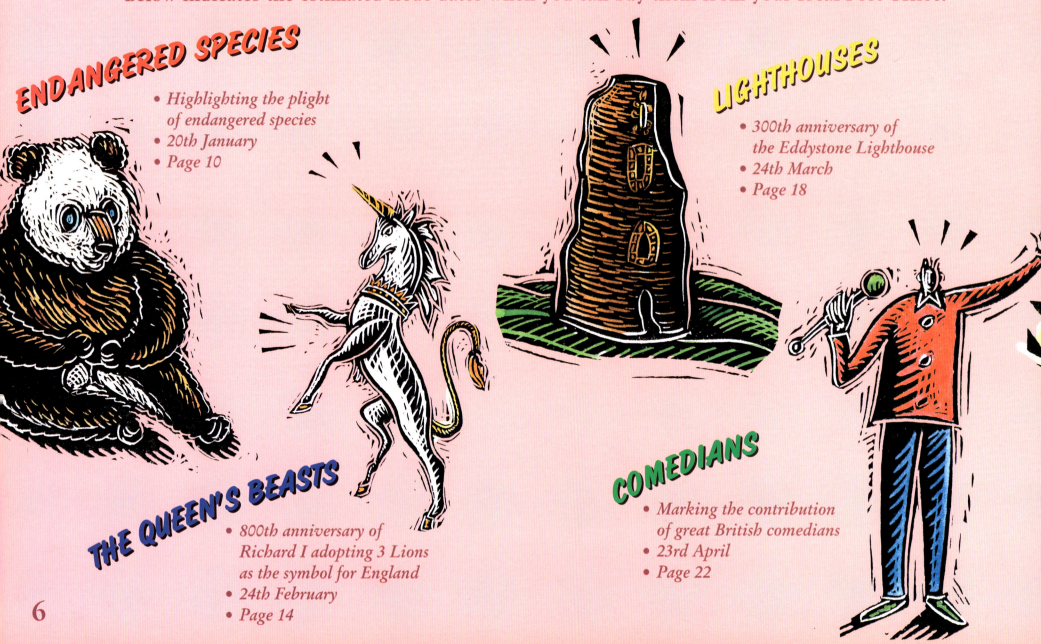

1998 Special Stamp Issues

This year there will be nine sets of Special Stamps released by Royal Mail.
Below indicates the estimated issue dates when you can buy them from your local Post Office.

ENDANGERED SPECIES
- Highlighting the plight of endangered species
- 20th January
- Page 10

THE QUEEN'S BEASTS
- 800th anniversary of Richard I adopting 3 Lions as the symbol for England
- 24th February
- Page 14

LIGHTHOUSES
- 300th anniversary of the Eddystone Lighthouse
- 24th March
- Page 18

COMEDIANS
- Marking the contribution of great British comedians
- 23rd April
- Page 22

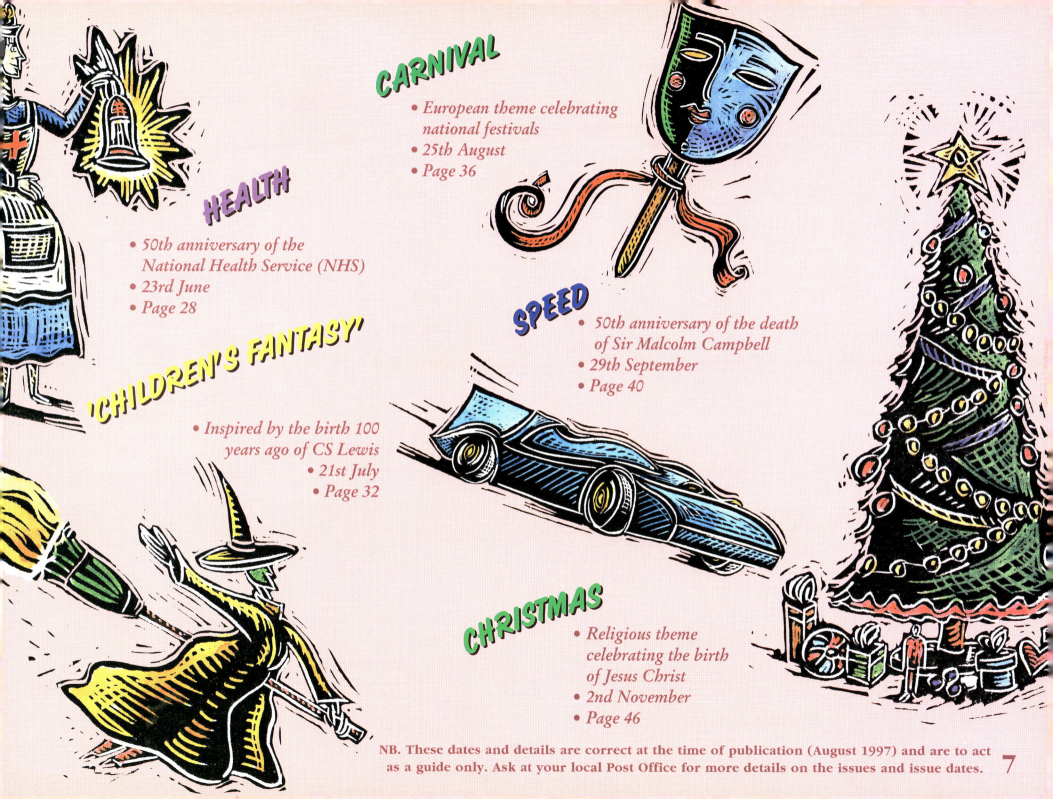

CARNIVAL
- European theme celebrating national festivals
- 25th August
- Page 36

HEALTH
- 50th anniversary of the National Health Service (NHS)
- 23rd June
- Page 28

'CHILDREN'S FANTASY'
- Inspired by the birth 100 years ago of CS Lewis
- 21st July
- Page 32

SPEED
- 50th anniversary of the death of Sir Malcolm Campbell
- 29th September
- Page 40

CHRISTMAS
- Religious theme celebrating the birth of Jesus Christ
- 2nd November
- Page 46

NB. These dates and details are correct at the time of publication (August 1997) and are to act as a guide only. Ask at your local Post Office for more details on the issues and issue dates.

How to Collect Stamps

British Special Stamps are amongst the most beautiful and interesting in the world. Collecting them is great fun and at the same time you can learn lots of amazing facts!

You can buy Special Stamps from your local Post Office - look out for the dates in the Annual when the stamps are issued.

Alternatively you may wish to buy your British stamps directly from the British Philatelic Bureau - call 0345 641 641 (Mon-Fri 8.30am-4.30pm) for more details.

You may wish to collect used stamps - simply collect them from letters you receive!

For more information on stamps and stamp collecting write to:- Royal Mail Collectors Club, Dept. 2734, Freepost NEA1431, SUNDERLAND, SR9 9XN

There are no rules on how to put your Special Stamps into the Annual, but here are a few general pointers:

If you wish you can simply stick them in, but it is better to use special gummed hinges which you can buy from your local stamp shop (look in your local directory under 'Stamp Dealers' for details of your nearest shop), or from major high street stationers.

The best way to display your stamps however, is to use clear protective mounts which you can also buy from your local stamp shop or from major high street stationers.

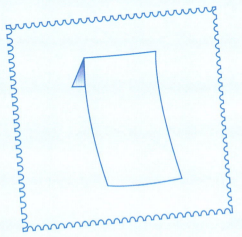

- *Lightly moisten the short top folded gummed portion of the hinge.*
- *Stick it carefully to the reverse side of the stamp, lightly above centre.*
- *Lightly moisten the long bottom gummed portion of the hinge and carefully stick it to the page.*
- *Never remove hinges from stamps while the hinge is still wet. You could damage both the page and stamp.*

Alternatively, to receive a full year's set of clear protective mounts and 15 FREE assorted used world stamps, simply send a cheque or postal order for £2.50 made payable to 'Complete Collections' together with your name and address clearly written in block capitals on a piece of paper, to: Stamp Mount Offer, Complete Collections Ltd, Oak Lodge, 8 Teasel Way, FERNDOWN, Dorset BH22 0PQ.

The clear protective mounts will be available after 23rd November 1997. Please allow 28 days for delivery after this date. Price includes postage, packing, stamp mounts and is inclusive of VAT.

ENDANGERED SPECIES

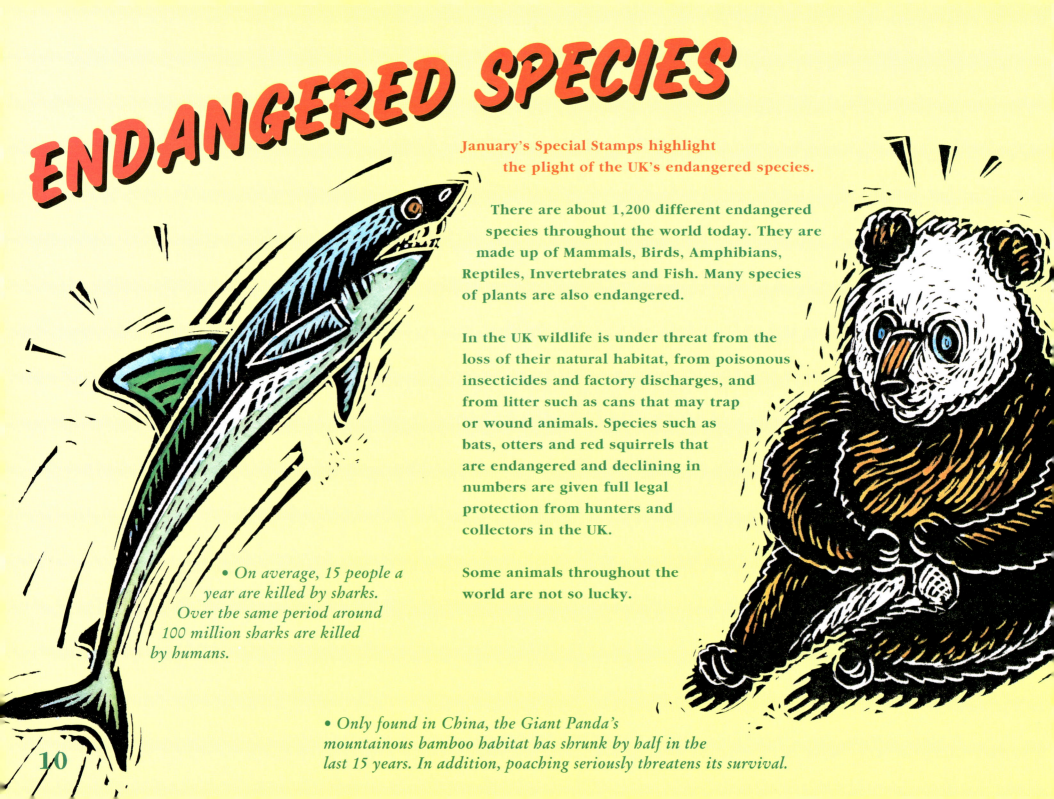

January's Special Stamps highlight the plight of the UK's endangered species.

There are about 1,200 different endangered species throughout the world today. They are made up of Mammals, Birds, Amphibians, Reptiles, Invertebrates and Fish. Many species of plants are also endangered.

In the UK wildlife is under threat from the loss of their natural habitat, from poisonous insecticides and factory discharges, and from litter such as cans that may trap or wound animals. Species such as bats, otters and red squirrels that are endangered and declining in numbers are given full legal protection from hunters and collectors in the UK.

Some animals throughout the world are not so lucky.

- On average, 15 people a year are killed by sharks. Over the same period around 100 million sharks are killed by humans.

- Only found in China, the Giant Panda's mountainous bamboo habitat has shrunk by half in the last 15 years. In addition, poaching seriously threatens its survival.

- *Tigers may be the first of many majestic species living today to become extinct because of demand for their body parts as traditional Oriental medicines.*

Date of issue **20th January 1998**
(Issue dates subject to change- ask at your local post office for more details)

JANUARY

1 Thursday — *New Year's Day*

2 Friday — *Bank Holiday (Scotland)*

3 Saturday

4 Sunday

5 Monday

6 Tuesday — *Epiphany*

7 Wednesday

8 Thursday

9 Friday

10 Saturday — *Ramadan Begins (Islamic)*

11 Sunday

12 Monday

13 Tuesday

14 Wednesday — *Romana's Birthday (1972)*

15 Thursday

16 Friday

17 Saturday

18 Sunday

19 Monday

20 Tuesday — **Endangered Species Special Stamps out today!**

21 Wednesday

22 Thursday

23 Friday

24 Saturday

25 Sunday — *Burns Night*

26 Monday

27 Tuesday

28 Wednesday — *Chinese New Year*

29 Thursday — *Chinese New Year/Eid Al-Fittr (Islamic)*

30 Friday — *Chinese New Year*

31 Saturday

13

THE QUEEN'S BEASTS

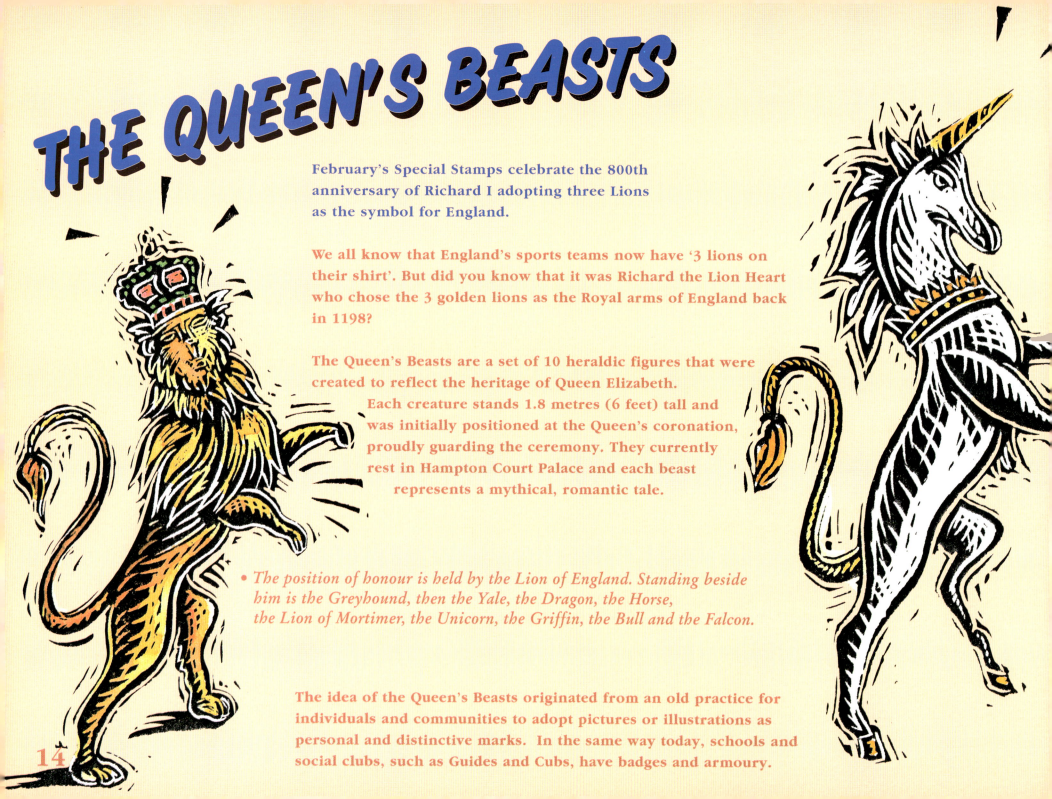

February's Special Stamps celebrate the 800th anniversary of Richard I adopting three Lions as the symbol for England.

We all know that England's sports teams now have '3 lions on their shirt'. But did you know that it was Richard the Lion Heart who chose the 3 golden lions as the Royal arms of England back in 1198?

The Queen's Beasts are a set of 10 heraldic figures that were created to reflect the heritage of Queen Elizabeth. Each creature stands 1.8 metres (6 feet) tall and was initially positioned at the Queen's coronation, proudly guarding the ceremony. They currently rest in Hampton Court Palace and each beast represents a mythical, romantic tale.

- *The position of honour is held by the Lion of England. Standing beside him is the Greyhound, then the Yale, the Dragon, the Horse, the Lion of Mortimer, the Unicorn, the Griffin, the Bull and the Falcon.*

The idea of the Queen's Beasts originated from an old practice for individuals and communities to adopt pictures or illustrations as personal and distinctive marks. In the same way today, schools and social clubs, such as Guides and Cubs, have badges and armoury.

Date of issue **24th February 1998**
(Issue dates subject to change- ask at your local post office for more details)

15

FEBRUARY

1 Sunday

2 Monday

3 Tuesday — Bonnie and Mabel's Birthday

4 Wednesday

5 Thursday

6 Friday — *Accession of Queen Elizabeth II (1952)*

7 Saturday

8 Sunday

9 Monday

10 Tuesday

11 Wednesday

12 Thursday

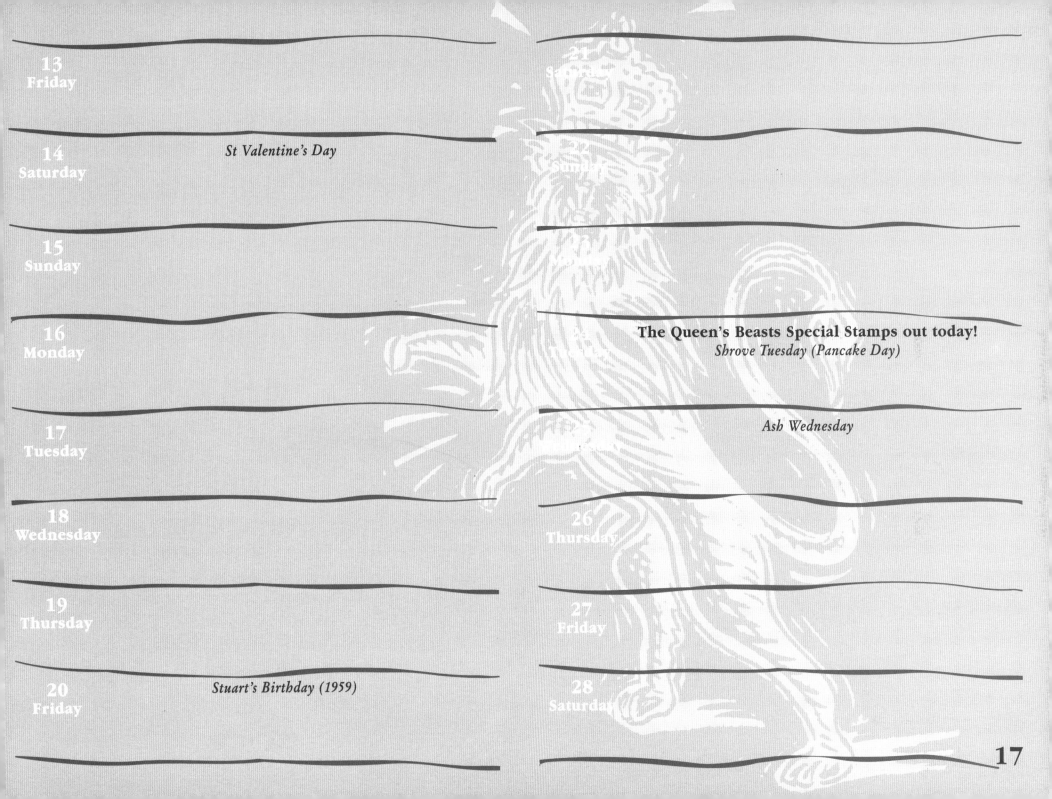

13 Friday

14 Saturday — *St Valentine's Day*

15 Sunday

16 Monday

17 Tuesday

18 Wednesday

19 Thursday

20 Friday — *Stuart's Birthday (1959)*

21 Saturday

22 Sunday

24 Tuesday — **The Queen's Beasts Special Stamps out today!** *Shrove Tuesday (Pancake Day)*

25 Wednesday — *Ash Wednesday*

26 Thursday

27 Friday

28 Saturday

17

LIGHTHOUSES

March's Special Stamps celebrate the 300th anniversary of the Eddystone Lighthouse.

Lighthouses are landmarks built to warn ships of dangerous rocky areas around coastal regions. The earliest recorded lighthouse 'Pharos of Alexandria' was built around 250BC on the island of Pharos, off the coast of Alexandria on the northern coast of Egypt. This lighthouse was the tallest stone building in the world until it was blown down during a terrible storm in 1326.

- The Pharos at Dover Castle that overlooks the harbour, was built by the Romans around the beginning of the second century AD. Originally the octagonal tower stood 24 metres high with a top platform on which a fire burned.

- The earliest British rock lighthouse was completed on Eddystone in Plymouth by Henry Winstanley in 1698. Unfortunately, the lighthouse and Winstanley were swept away during a storm in 1703.

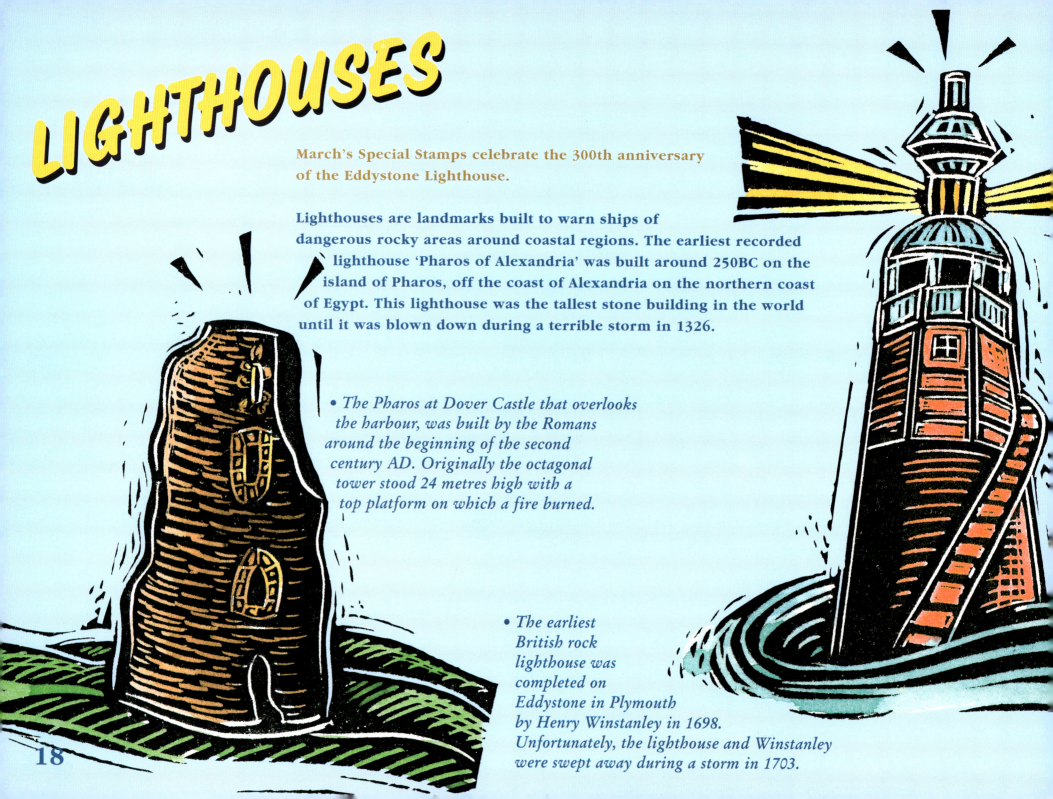

- *Today the majority of lighthouses are controlled automatically, with remote control light and fog signals. Most have computers that can analyse the weather conditions and transmit the information to stations in-shore.*

Date of issue **24th March 1998**

(Issue dates subject to change- ask at your local post office for more details)

MARCH

1 Sunday — St David's Day (Wales)

2 Monday

3 Tuesday

4 Wednesday

5 Thursday

6 Friday

7 Saturday

8 Sunday — International Women's Day

9 Monday — Commonwealth Day

10 Tuesday

11 Wednesday — National No Smoking Day

12 Thursday — Holi (Hindu)

13 Friday

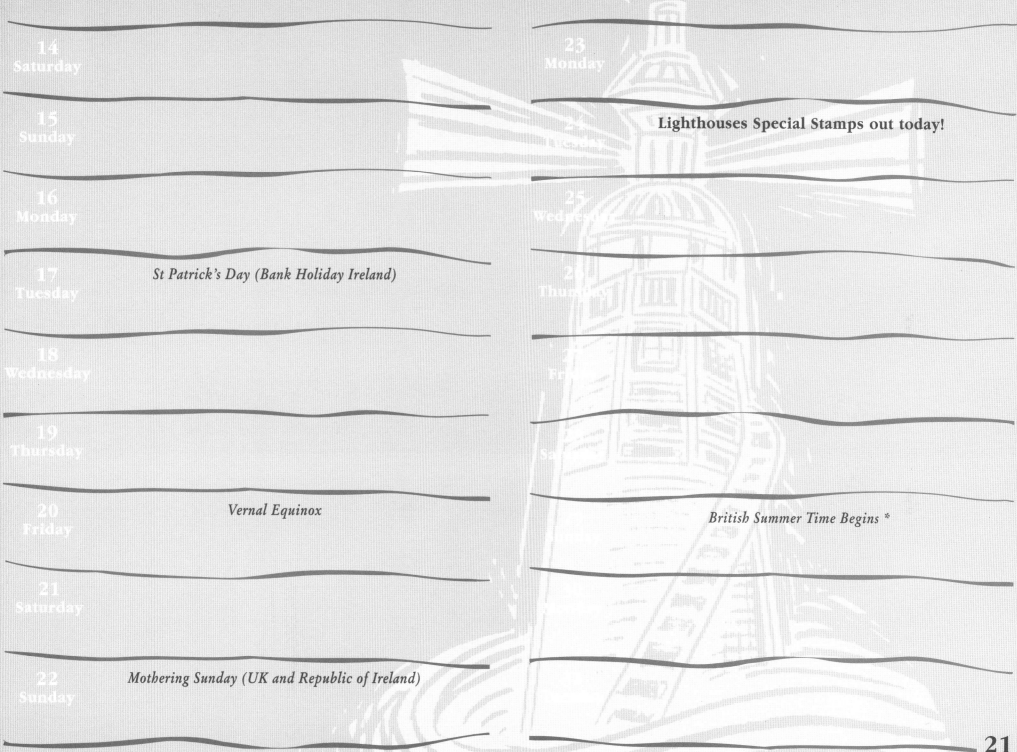

14 Saturday

15 Sunday

16 Monday

17 Tuesday — St Patrick's Day (Bank Holiday Ireland)

18 Wednesday

19 Thursday

20 Friday — Vernal Equinox

21 Saturday

22 Sunday — Mothering Sunday (UK and Republic of Ireland)

23 Monday

24 Tuesday — Lighthouses Special Stamps out today!

25 Wednesday

26 Thursday

27 Friday

28 Saturday

29 Sunday — British Summer Time Begins *

* Subject to confirmation

COMEDIANS

April's Special Stamps mark the contribution of great British comedians.

There are numerous forms of comedy including stand-up, slap stick, tragedy, musical and black humour. Humour is very personal and everyone has their own likes and dislikes. Making people laugh is an art form and Great Britain has produced some of the most talented comedians in the world. Some of our earliest comedians were clowns.

Did you know that clowns have been around since the 1500's? In Britain the first professional clown was Richard Tarleton. He was well known for his *"Jig"* which was a funny rhyme, sung and danced to popular tunes.

Born in 1778, Joseph Grimaldi was the most famous of all British clowns. He created the clown costume still used today: wide trousers, tufts of hair on a bald wig and a white face with a red triangle on each cheek.

Many of Britain's favourite comedians of recent years have had their own catch-phrase - '*Just Like That*' (Tommy Cooper) and '*Alwight*' (Michael Barrymore). Can you think of any other comedians who have their own catch-phrases today?

Some of the funniest people on television today are comedy actors or actresses who make us laugh playing someone else - Rowan Atkinson as Mr Bean, Harry Enfield as 'Kevin' and Caroline Aherne as Mrs Merton.

Date of issue **23rd April 1998**
(Issue dates subject to change- ask at your local post office for more details)

APRIL

1 Wednesday — April Fools Day

2 Thursday

3 Friday

4 Saturday

5 Sunday — Palm Sunday

6 Monday

7 Tuesday — World Health Day / Eid Al-Addha (Islamic)

8 Wednesday

9 Thursday — Maundy Thursday

10 Friday — Good Friday (UK)

11 Saturday — Jewish Passover

12 Sunday — Easter Day

13 Monday	*Easter Monday (UK and Republic of Ireland)*
14 Tuesday	*Cuckoo Day*
15 Wednesday	*Swallow Day / Katy's Birthday (1971)*
16 Thursday	
17 Friday	
18 Saturday	
19 Sunday	*Primrose Day*
20 Monday	
21 Tuesday	*Birthday of Queen Elizabeth II (1926)*

22 Wednesday	
23 Thursday	**Comedians Special Stamps out today!** *St George's Day (England)*
24 Friday	*St Mark's Eve*
25 Saturday	
26 Sunday	
27 Monday	*Al-Hijra (Islamic New Year)*
28 Tuesday	
29 Wednesday	
30 Thursday	

MAY

1 Friday — May Day

2 Saturday

3 Sunday

4 Monday — May Day Holiday (UK and Republic of Ireland)

5 Tuesday

6 Wednesday — Penny Black issued today in 1840

7 Thursday

8 Friday — VE Day (1945) / World Red Cross Day

9 Saturday — Liberation Day (Channel Islands)

10 Sunday

11 Monday — Wesak Day (Buddhist)

12 Tuesday

13 Wednesday

14 Thursday — Mallard Day

15 Friday

16 Saturday

17 Sunday

18 Monday

19 Tuesday

20 Wednesday — Ascension Day

21 Thursday

23 Saturday

24 Sunday

25 Monday — Spring Holiday (UK)

27 Wednesday

28 Thursday

29 Friday — Royal Oak Day / Martyrdom of Guru Arjan Dev Ji (Sikh)

30 Saturday

31 Sunday — Shavuot (Jewish Pentecost) / Whit Sunday

27

HEALTH

June's, Special Stamps celebrate the 50th anniversary of the National Health Service (NHS).

The National Health Service, pioneered in 1948 by Aneurin Bevan, Minister of Health, offered free medical, dental and hospital services to everyone. Today adults have to pay for prescriptions and for both dental and eye care.

Alexander Fleming (1881-1944) discovered penicillin in 1928. This was the first mass produced antibiotic.

During an average day in England, there will be approximately 700,000 people who visit their doctor, 1,500,000 prescriptions will be dispensed by pharmacies and 100,000 people will have a dental check up. Additionally, 90,000 people will obtain care from a hospital outpatient clinic and 1,700 babies will be born.

More than 9,500 people give blood daily.

The NHS has a yearly budget of approximately £41 billion and employs nearly 1,000,000 people. This makes it Europe's largest employer.

- Florence Nightingale (1820-1910) set the standards for modern nursing. She began nursing in Harley Street Hospital, London and later managed the nursing of the wounded soldiers in the Crimean War. After the war, Florence founded the first professional school of nursing at St Thomas's Hospital, London.

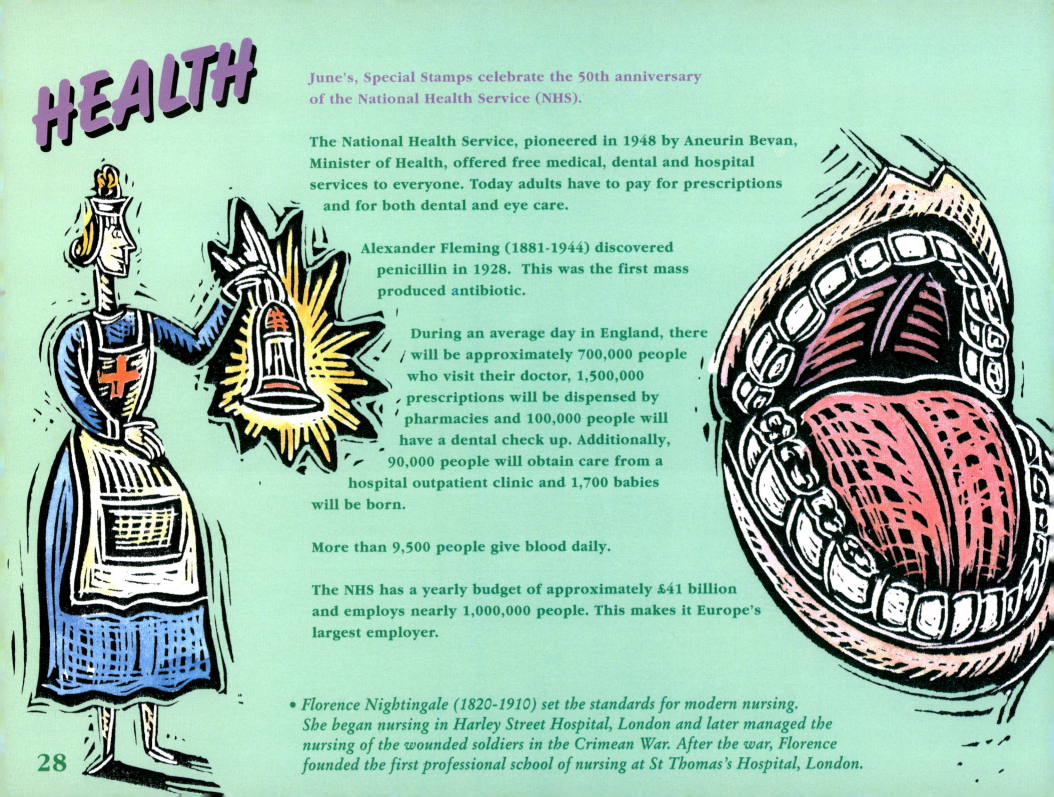

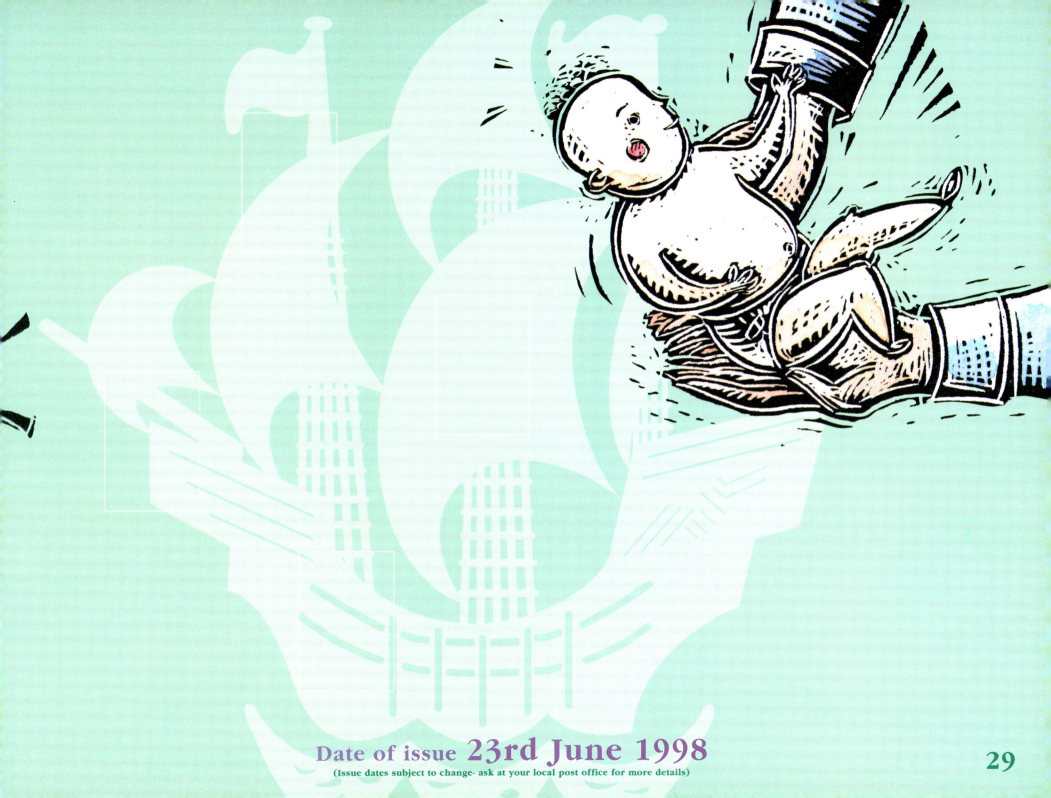

Date of issue **23rd June 1998**
(Issue dates subject to change- ask at your local post office for more details)

JUNE

5 Friday

6 Saturday — D-Day (1944)

7 Sunday

8 Monday

9 Tuesday

10 Wednesday — Birthday of Duke of Edinburgh (1921)

11 Thursday — Corpus Christi

12 Friday

Coronation Day (1953)

15 Saturday

Official Birthday of Queen Elizabeth II

16 Sunday

17 Monday

18 Tuesday

Battle of Waterloo (1815)

19 Wednesday

20 Thursday

21 Friday

Father's Day (UK, Ireland, USA, Canada) / Longest Day

22 Monday

Health Special Stamps out today!
Midsummer's Eve

Midsummer's Day / St John the Baptist Day

'CHILDREN'S FANTASY'

July's Special Stamps are inspired by the birth of CS Lewis 100 years ago.

Born Clive Staples Lewis (1898-1963), he was a British scholar, novelist and author. As an author Lewis reached a wide range of readers in three different areas: academics, religion and children's stories.

He wrote the series of seven children's books under the title, 'The Chronicles of Narnia', starting with 'The Lion, the Witch and the Wardrobe' in 1950 and finishing with 'The Last Battle' in 1956.

CS Lewis also wrote 'The Screwtape Letters' and aimed to teach the reader about the Christian faith. There are 31 letters in which an elderly, experienced devil named Screwtape educates his junior, Wormwood, in the art of tempting and converting Christians.

One of Lewis's best science fiction novels, 'The Cosmic Trilogy' tells the story of an English linguist called Ransom who travels to Mars and Venus and becomes involved in a cosmic struggle between good and evil in the solar system.

Date of issue **21st July 1998**
(Issue dates subject to change- ask at your local post office for more details)

33

JULY

1 Wednesday

2 Thursday

3 Friday

4 Saturday

5 Sunday — Tynwald Day (Isle of Man)

6 Monday — Milad Al-Nabi (Prophet's Birthday-Islamic)

7 Tuesday

8 Wednesday

9 Thursday — Dharma Day (Buddhist)

10 Friday

11 Saturday

12 Sunday — Orangeman's Day

13 Monday

St Swithin's Day

St James's Day

Children's Fantasy Special Stamps out today!

CARNIVAL

August's Special Stamps celebrate European national festivals...Carnival!

The term 'carnival' originated from the Roman Catholics who celebrated during the final few days before Lent. Roman Catholics originally stopped eating meat for 40 days, but nowadays they can choose to give up any particular food. The first day of the carnival varies from country to country, but usually celebrations begin on Shrove Tuesday.

- One of the world's most famous carnivals takes place in Rio de Janiero, Brazil. This is a masque ball where people dress in elaborate costumes and parade through the streets.

- The Notting Hill Carnival in London first began in 1966 as a local event. It has grown and developed over the years and is now one of Britain's largest festivals. The theme of the carnival is based upon the carnivals in the Caribbean; again, people dress up in costumes and parade through the streets.

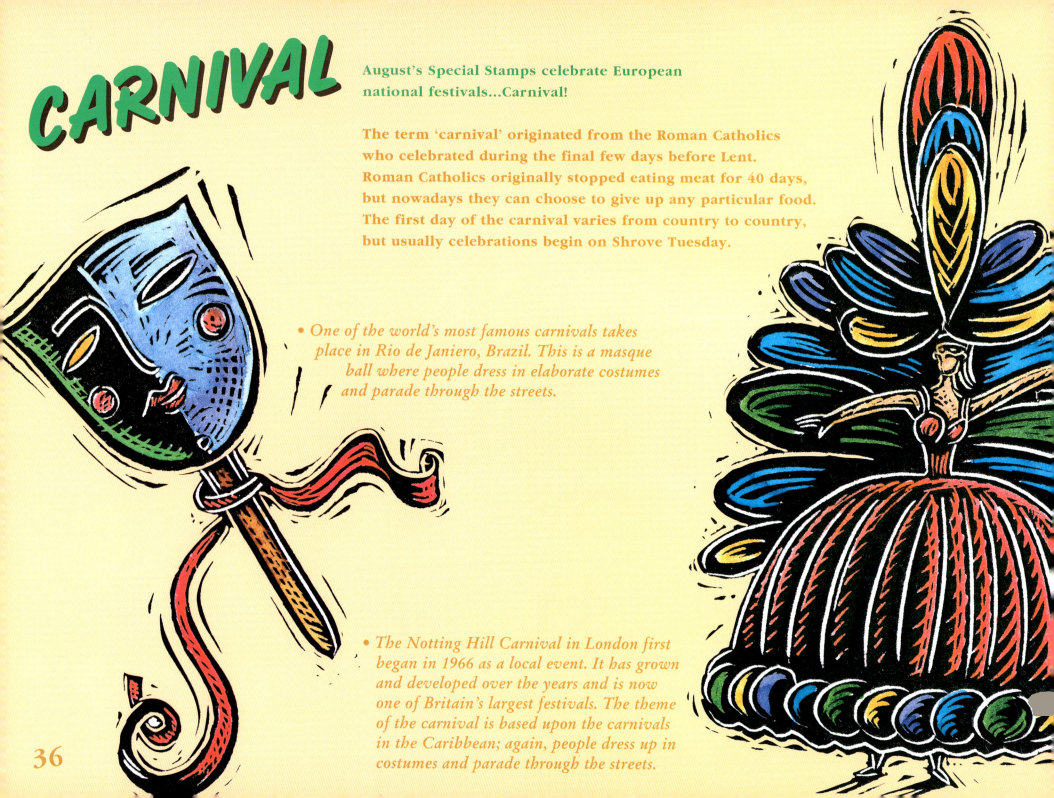

- Another famous carnival is the 'Mardi Gras' which takes place in New Orleans, USA. Mardi Gras actually means 'Fat Tuesday' and is when all the fat is eaten in the house before Lent commences.

Date of issue **25th August 1998**
(Issue dates subject to change- ask at your local post office for more details)

AUGUST

1 Saturday

2 Sunday

3 Monday — *Holiday (Republic of Ireland and Scotland)*

4 Tuesday — *Birthday of Queen Elizabeth the Queen Mother (1900)*

5 Wednesday

6 Thursday — *Hiroshima Day*

7 Friday

8 Saturday

9 Sunday

10 Monday

11 Tuesday

12 Wednesday

13 Thursday

VJ Day (1945)

Carnival Special Stamps out today!

Notting Hill Carnival

Late Summer Holiday (UK) / Notting Hill Carnival

39

SPEED

September's Special Stamps commemorate the 50th anniversary of the death of Sir Malcolm Campbell.

The one-mile land speed record is held by Richard Noble, in *Thrust 2*, with a speed of 1,019.467 km/h (633.468 mph) that is one mile in 5.683 seconds. The record took place in Black Rock Desert, Nevada, USA on 4th October, 1983.

Did you know that according to Dr Johnson's theory in the 18th century, it was considered that a man would suffocate if he drove faster than 20mph! This theory was believed until the invention of the steam locomotive in the 19th century.

- Did you know that a Formula 1 car can go from 0 mph to 100 mph and back to 0 mph in under 6 seconds? Plus, a Formula 1 driver can lose up to 2 litres of body fluids during a race!

- Sir Malcolm Campbell (1885-1948) was a racing driver who set many early land and water speed records. He increased the land speed record from 235 km/h (146 mph) in 1924 to 484 km/h (301 mph) in 1935, in a car called 'Bluebird'.

- *The world airspeed record is 3,529.56 km/h (2,193.17 mph) achieved in a Lockheed SR-71A 'Blackbird' over a 25 km (15.5 mile) course near Beale Air Force Base in California, USA on 28th July 1976.*

Date of issue **29th September 1998**
(Issue dates subject to change- ask at your local post office for more details)

SEPTEMBER

1 Tuesday

2 Wednesday

3 Thursday

4 Friday

5 Saturday

6 Sunday

7 Monday

8 Tuesday

9 Wednesday

10 Thursday

11 Friday

12 Saturday

13 Sunday

14 Monday

15 Tuesday — *Battle of Britain Day (1940)*

16 Wednesday

17 Thursday

18 Friday

19 Saturday

20 Sunday

21 Monday — *Navratri (Hindu) / Rosh Hashanah (Jewish New Year-5761)*

22 Tuesday

23 Wednesday — *Autumn Equinox*

24 Thursday

25 Friday

26 Saturday — *Grandparents' Day*

27 Sunday

28 Monday

29 Tuesday — **Speed Special Stamps out today!**

30 Wednesday — *Yom Kippur (Day of Atonement - Jewish)*

OCTOBER

1 Thursday

2 Friday

3 Saturday

4 Sunday

5 Monday
Succoth (Tabernacles - Jewish)

6 Tuesday

7 Wednesday

8 Thursday

9 Friday

10 Saturday

11 Sunday

12 Monday

13 Tuesday

14 Wednesday — Battle of Hastings (1066)

15 Thursday

16 Friday — **Blue Peter's 40th Birthday! (1958)**

17 Saturday

18 Sunday

19 Monday — *Diwali (Hindu)*

20

21 — *Trafalgar Day (1805)*

22 Thursday

23 Friday

24 Saturday — *United Nations Day*

25 Sunday — *St Crispin's Day / British Summer Time Ends**

26 Monday

27

28

29

30

31 Saturday — *Hallowe'en*

* Subject to confirmation

CHRISTMAS

November's Special Stamps mark the birth of Jesus Christ and the festival of Christmas.

Christmas originates from two sources, both celebrating the return to health of the sun after its shortest day. Roman Emperors chose December 25th as the birthday of the unconquered sun and pagan tribes from northern Europe held a 12-day winter festival called Yule, with trees and mistletoe. Christianity adopted and adapted both festivities into Christmas celebrating the birth of Jesus Christ.

The best-known Christmas tree in Britain is the one in Trafalgar Square. Since 1947 this tree has been a yearly gift from the people of Norway. It is in tribute to the friendship which the two nations shared during World War II.

The first Christmas card was designed by John Callcott Horsley in 1843. One thousand copies were printed. The card featured a happy family gathering. This caused offence to some people, however, as the children were pictured with wine glasses!

Since 1932, when George V spoke to the people on the radio, the King or Queen's message at 3pm has been an important part of Christmas Day.

Date of issue 2nd November 1998
(Issue dates subject to change- ask at your local post office for more details)

NOVEMBER

1 Sunday — *All Saints' Day*

2 Monday — **Christmas Special Stamps out today!** *All Souls' Day*

3 Tuesday

4 Wednesday — *Birthday of Guru Nanak Dev Ji (Sikh)*

5 Thursday — *Guy Fawkes' Night*

6 Friday

7 Saturday

8 Sunday — *Remembrance Sunday*

9 Monday

10 Tuesday

11 Wednesday — *Armistice Day (1918)*

12 Thursday

| 13 Friday |

| 14 Saturday | Birthday of the Prince of Wales (1948) |

| 15 Sunday |

| 16 Monday |

| 17 Tuesday |

| 18 Wednesday |

| 19 Thursday |

| 20 Friday |

| 21 Saturday |

| 22 Sunday |

Martyrdom of Guru Tegh Bahadur Ji (Sikh)

St Andrew's Day (Scotland) / Richard's Birthday (1975)

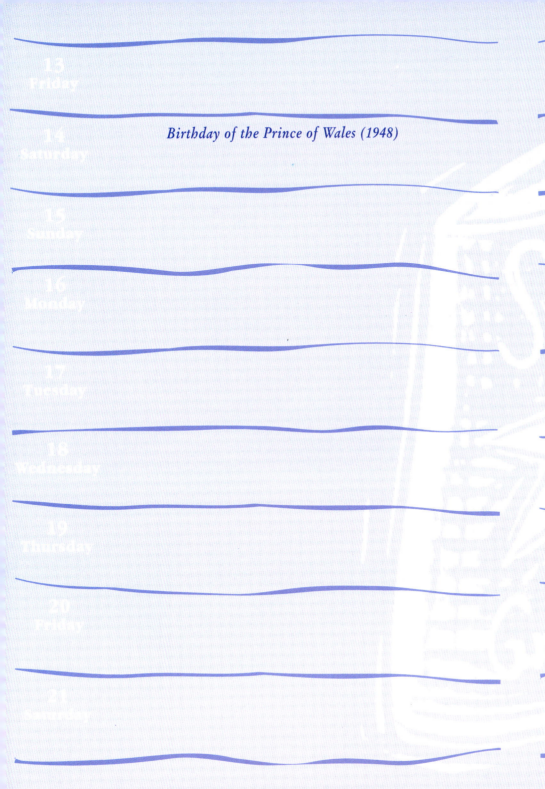

DECEMBER

1 Tuesday

2 Wednesday

3 Thursday

4 Friday

5 Saturday

6 Sunday

7 Monday

8 Tuesday

9 Wednesday

10 Thursday — *Human Rights Day*

11 Friday

12 Saturday

13 Sunday

14 Monday — *Hanukkah (Jewish)*

15 Tuesday

16 Wednesday

17 Thursday

18 Friday

19 Saturday

20 Sunday

21 Monday

22 Tuesday — *Shortest Day*

23 Wednesday

24 Thursday — *Christmas Eve*

25 Friday — *Christmas Day / Birthday of Guru Gobind Singh Ji (Sikh)*

26 Saturday — *Boxing Day (UK) / St Steven's Day (Republic of Ireland)*

General Stamp Collecting Pages

*Use these next 8 pages to collect your other stamps, from Great Britain and around the world.
Why not separate your pages into countries or perhaps into different subjects (for example, animals or flowers).*

Special Names and Addresses

Keep the names, addresses and telephone numbers of your friends and family here for quick reference.

Name: _____	Name: _____	Name: _____
Address: _____	Address: _____	Address: _____
_____	_____	_____
Postcode: _____ ☎ _____	Postcode: _____ ☎ _____	Postcode: _____ ☎ _____
Name: _____	Name: _____	Name: _____
Address: _____	Address: _____	Address: _____
_____	_____	_____
Postcode: _____ ☎ _____	Postcode: _____ ☎ _____	Postcode: _____ ☎ _____
Name: _____	Name: _____	Name: _____
Address: _____	Address: _____	Address: _____
_____	_____	_____
Postcode: _____ ☎ _____	Postcode: _____ ☎ _____	Postcode: _____ ☎ _____

Name:	Name:	Name:
Address:	Address:	Address:
Postcode: ☎	Postcode: ☎	Postcode: ☎
Name:	Name:	Name:
Address:	Address:	Address:
Postcode: ☎	Postcode: ☎	Postcode: ☎
Name:	Name:	Name:
Address:	Address:	Address:
Postcode: ☎	Postcode: ☎	Postcode: ☎
Name:	Name:	Name:
Address:	Address:	Address:
Postcode: ☎	Postcode: ☎	Postcode: ☎

Name:	Name:	Name:
Address:	Address:	Address:
Postcode: ☎	Postcode: ☎	Postcode: ☎
Name:	Name:	Name:
Address:	Address:	Address:
Postcode: ☎	Postcode: ☎	Postcode: ☎
Name:	Name:	Name:
Address:	Address:	Address:
Postcode: ☎	Postcode: ☎	Postcode: ☎
Name:	Name:	Name:
Address:	Address:	Address:
Postcode: ☎	Postcode: ☎	Postcode: ☎

Name: _____	Name: _____	Name: _____
Address: _____	Address: _____	Address: _____
_____	_____	_____
Postcode: _____ ☎ _____	Postcode: _____ ☎ _____	Postcode: _____ ☎ _____
Name: _____	Name: _____	Name: _____
Address: _____	Address: _____	Address: _____
_____	_____	_____
Postcode: _____ ☎ _____	Postcode: _____ ☎ _____	Postcode: _____ ☎ _____
Name: _____	Name: _____	Name: _____
Address: _____	Address: _____	Address: _____
_____	_____	_____
Postcode: _____ ☎ _____	Postcode: _____ ☎ _____	Postcode: _____ ☎ _____
Name: _____	Name: _____	Name: _____
Address: _____	Address: _____	Address: _____
_____	_____	_____
Postcode: _____ ☎ _____	Postcode: _____ ☎ _____	Postcode: _____ ☎ _____

Notes

Notes

67

Notes

January

Monday		5	12	19	26	
Tuesday		6	13	20	27	
Wednesday		7	14	21	28	
Thursday	1	8	15	22	29	
Friday	2	9	16	23	30	
Saturday	3	10	17	24	31	
Sunday	4	11	18	25		

February

Monday		2	9	16	23
Tuesday		3	10	17	24
Wednesday		4	11	18	25
Thursday		5	12	19	26
Friday		6	13	20	27
Saturday		7	14	21	28
Sunday	1	8	15	22	

March

Monday		2	9	16	23	30
Tuesday		3	10	17	24	31
Wednesday		4	11	18	25	
Thursday		5	12	19	26	
Friday		6	13	20	27	
Saturday		7	14	21	28	
Sunday	1	8	15	22	29	

April

Monday		6	13	20	27
Tuesday		7	14	21	28
Wednesday	1	8	15	22	29
Thursday	2	9	16	23	30
Friday	3	10	17	24	
Saturday	4	11	18	25	
Sunday	5	12	19	26	

May

Monday		4	11	18	25
Tuesday		5	12	19	26
Wednesday		6	13	20	27
Thursday		7	14	21	28
Friday	1	8	15	22	29
Saturday	2	9	16	23	30
Sunday	3	10	17	24	31

June

Monday	1	8	15	22	29
Tuesday	2	9	16	23	30
Wednesday	3	10	17	24	
Thursday	4	11	18	25	
Friday	5	12	19	26	
Saturday	6	13	20	27	
Sunday	7	14	21	28	

July

Monday		6	13	20	27
Tuesday		7	14	21	28
Wednesday	1	8	15	22	29
Thursday	2	9	16	23	30
Friday	3	10	17	24	31
Saturday	4	11	18	25	
Sunday	5	12	19	26	

August

Monday		3	10	17	24	31
Tuesday		4	11	18	25	
Wednesday		5	12	19	26	
Thursday		6	13	20	27	
Friday		7	14	21	28	
Saturday	1	8	15	22	29	
Sunday	2	9	16	23	30	

September

Monday		7	14	21	28
Tuesday	1	8	15	22	29
Wednesday	2	9	16	23	30
Thursday	3	10	17	24	
Friday	4	11	18	25	
Saturday	5	12	19	26	
Sunday	6	13	20	27	

October

Monday		5	12	19	26
Tuesday		6	13	20	27
Wednesday		7	14	21	28
Thursday	1	8	15	22	29
Friday	2	9	16	23	30
Saturday	3	10	17	24	31
Sunday	4	11	18	25	

November

Monday		2	9	16	23	30
Tuesday		3	10	17	24	
Wednesday		4	11	18	25	
Thursday		5	12	19	26	
Friday		6	13	20	27	
Saturday		7	14	21	28	
Sunday	1	8	15	22	29	

December

Monday		7	14	21	28
Tuesday	1	8	15	22	29
Wednesday	2	9	16	23	30
Thursday	3	10	17	24	31
Friday	4	11	18	25	
Saturday	5	12	19	26	
Sunday	6	13	20	27	

January

Monday		6	13	20	27
Tuesday		7	14	21	28
Wednesday	1	8	15	22	29
Thursday	2	9	16	23	30
Friday	3	10	17	24	31
Saturday	4	11	18	25	
Sunday	5	12	19	26	

February

Monday		3	10	17	24
Tuesday		4	11	18	25
Wednesday		5	12	19	26
Thursday		6	13	20	27
Friday		7	14	21	28
Saturday	1	8	15	22	
Sunday	2	9	16	23	

March

Monday		3	10	17	24	31
Tuesday		4	11	18	25	
Wednesday		5	12	19	26	
Thursday		6	13	20	27	
Friday		7	14	21	28	
Saturday	1	8	15	22	29	
Sunday	2	9	16	23	30	

April

Monday		7	14	21	28
Tuesday	1	8	15	22	29
Wednesday	2	9	16	23	30
Thursday	3	10	17	24	
Friday	4	11	18	25	
Saturday	5	12	19	26	
Sunday	6	13	20	27	

May

Monday		5	12	19	26
Tuesday		6	13	20	27
Wednesday		7	14	21	28
Thursday	1	8	15	22	29
Friday	2	9	16	23	30
Saturday	3	10	17	24	31
Sunday	4	11	18	25	

June

Monday		2	9	16	23	30
Tuesday		3	10	17	24	
Wednesday		4	11	18	25	
Thursday		5	12	19	26	
Friday		6	13	20	27	
Saturday		7	14	21	28	
Sunday	1	8	15	22	29	

July

Monday		7	14	21	28
Tuesday	1	8	15	22	29
Wednesday	2	9	16	23	30
Thursday	3	10	17	24	31
Friday	4	11	18	25	
Saturday	5	12	19	26	
Sunday	6	13	20	27	

August

Monday		4	11	18	25
Tuesday		5	12	19	26
Wednesday		6	13	20	27
Thursday		7	14	21	28
Friday	1	8	15	22	29
Saturday	2	9	16	23	30
Sunday	3	10	17	24	31

September

Monday	1	8	15	22	29
Tuesday	2	9	16	23	30
Wednesday	3	10	17	24	
Thursday	4	11	18	25	
Friday	5	12	19	26	
Saturday	6	13	20	27	
Sunday	7	14	21	28	

October

Monday		6	13	20	27
Tuesday		7	14	21	28
Wednesday	1	8	15	22	29
Thursday	2	9	16	23	30
Friday	3	10	17	24	31
Saturday	4	11	18	25	
Sunday	5	12	19	26	

November

Monday		3	10	17	24
Tuesday		4	11	18	25
Wednesday		5	12	19	26
Thursday		6	13	20	27
Friday		7	14	21	28
Saturday	1	8	15	22	29
Sunday	2	9	16	23	30

December

Monday	1	8	15	22	29
Tuesday	2	9	16	23	30
Wednesday	3	10	17	24	31
Thursday	4	11	18	25	
Friday	5	12	19	26	
Saturday	6	13	20	27	
Sunday	7	14	21	28	

January

Monday		4	11	18	25
Tuesday		5	12	19	26
Wednesday		6	13	20	27
Thursday		7	14	21	28
Friday	1	8	15	22	29
Saturday	2	9	16	23	30
Sunday	3	10	17	24	31

February

Monday	1	8	15	22
Tuesday	2	9	16	23
Wednesday	3	10	17	24
Thursday	4	11	18	25
Friday	5	12	19	26
Saturday	6	13	20	27
Sunday	7	14	21	28

March

Monday	1	8	15	22	29
Tuesday	2	9	16	23	30
Wednesday	3	10	17	24	31
Thursday	4	11	18	25	
Friday	5	12	19	26	
Saturday	6	13	20	27	
Sunday	7	14	21	28	

April

Monday		5	12	19	26
Tuesday		6	13	20	27
Wednesday		7	14	21	28
Thursday	1	8	15	22	29
Friday	2	9	16	23	30
Saturday	3	10	17	24	
Sunday	4	11	18	25	

May

Monday		3	10	17	24	31
Tuesday		4	11	18	25	
Wednesday		5	12	19	26	
Thursday		6	13	20	27	
Friday		7	14	21	28	
Saturday	1	8	15	22	29	
Sunday	2	9	16	23	30	

June

Monday		7	14	21	28
Tuesday	1	8	15	22	29
Wednesday	2	9	16	23	30
Thursday	3	10	17	24	
Friday	4	11	18	25	
Saturday	5	12	19	26	
Sunday	6	13	20	27	

July

Monday		5	12	19	26
Tuesday		6	13	20	27
Wednesday		7	14	21	28
Thursday	1	8	15	22	29
Friday	2	9	16	23	30
Saturday	3	10	17	24	31
Sunday	4	11	18	25	

August

Monday	2	9	16	23	30
Tuesday	3	10	17	24	31
Wednesday	4	11	18	25	
Thursday	5	12	19	26	
Friday	6	13	20	27	
Saturday	7	14	21	28	
Sunday	1	8	15	22	29

September

Monday		6	13	20	27
Tuesday		7	14	21	28
Wednesday	1	8	15	22	29
Thursday	2	9	16	23	30
Friday	3	10	17	24	
Saturday	4	11	18	25	
Sunday	5	12	19	26	

October

Monday		4	11	18	25
Tuesday		5	12	19	26
Wednesday		6	13	20	27
Thursday		7	14	21	28
Friday	1	8	15	22	29
Saturday	2	9	16	23	30
Sunday	3	10	17	24	31

November

Monday	1	8	15	22	29
Tuesday	2	9	16	23	30
Wednesday	3	10	17	24	
Thursday	4	11	18	25	
Friday	5	12	19	26	
Saturday	6	13	20	27	
Sunday	7	14	21	28	

December

Monday		6	13	20	27
Tuesday		7	14	21	28
Wednesday	1	8	15	22	29
Thursday	2	9	16	23	30
Friday	3	10	17	24	31
Saturday	4	11	18	25	
Sunday	5	12	19	26	

Acknowledgements

The Publishers wish to thank the following for their help in providing
information and assistance in the publication of the Blue Peter Stamp Annual:
Oliver Macfarlane, Anne Dixon and all the Blue Peter Team
including Stuart, Katy, Romana and Richard,
and BBC photographer Chris Capstick.
All at the Royal Mail Philatelic Department, especially Julietta Edgar and Rosena Robson.
Charles Letts & Company. Hampton Court Palace and WWF-UK.

The Publishers acknowledge their indebtedness to the following books and journals,
consulted for reference:
Lighthouses, Lynn F. Pearson (Shire Publications Ltd)
Encyclopaedia of Britain, Bamber Gasgoine (Macmillan)
The Guinness Book of Records (Guinness Publishing Ltd)
The Guinness Book of Theatre Facts & Feats, Michael Billington (Guinness Superlatives Ltd)
A Guide to the National Health Service, Department of Health
(NHS Executive Communications Unit)
Field Guide to Animals of Britain (Readers Digest)